Lea's Birthday

by Jay Dale
illustrated by Amanda Gulliver

"It is my birthday today!"
said Lea.

"Yes," said Dad.
"Happy birthday!"

"I am not going to school,"
said Lea.
"I will play at home
with you today."

Dad looked at Lea.

"You like going to school,"

he said.

"No," said Lea.
"I will play at home
with you today."

"The boys and girls
at school will look for you,"
said Dad.
"Your teacher will look
for you, too."

“Come on,” said Dad.
“You can go to school
with me.”

Lea went to school
with Dad.
She got out of the car
and went inside.

"Happy birthday!"
shouted all the boys
and girls.

Lea looked at the balloons.
"Thank you!" she said.

"We have a birthday hat
for you," said the teacher.

"We have a birthday cake
for you, too!"
said all the boys and girls.

2+2=4
4+1=5

“Happy birthday, Lea!”
shouted the boys and girls.